Children's Authors

Stan and Jan Berenstain

Mae Woods

ABDO Publishing Company

visit us at
www.abdopub.com

Published by ABDO Publishing Company, 4940 Viking Drive, Suite 622, Edina, Minnesota 55435. Copyright © 2000 Abdo Consulting Group, Inc., Pentagon Tower, P.O. Box 36036, Minneapolis, Minnesota 55435 USA. International copyrights reserved in all countries. No part of this book may be reproduced in any form without written permission from the publisher.

Published 2000
Printed in the United States of America
Second Printing 2002

Photos: Courtesy of Stan and Jan Berenstain
Editors: Bob Italia, Tamara L. Britton, Kate A. Furlong
Art Direction: Pat Laurel

Library of Congress Cataloging-in-Publication Data

Woods, Mae.
    Stan and Jan Berenstain / Mae Woods.
      p. cm. -- (Children's Authors)
    Includes bibliographical references (p.) and index.
    Summary: Describes the personal lives and professional development of the couple responsible for the Berenstain Bears books.
    ISBN 1-57765-115-4
    1. Berenstain, Stan, 1923---Juvenile literature. 2. Berenstain, Jan, 1923---Juvenile literature. 3. Authors, American--20th century--Biography--Juvenile literature. 4. Children's stories--Authorship--Juvenile literature. [1. Berenstain, Stan, 1923- 2. Berenstain, Jan, 1923- 3. Authors, American.] I. Title.

PS3552.E6997 Z96 2000
813'.5409--dc21
[B]
                                      00-036185

Contents

The Berenstain Team 4

Stan Berenstain.. 6

Jan Berenstain 8

Early Work.. 10

It's All in the Family... 12

The Birth of the Bears 14

About the Bears 16

Working Together 18

The Berenstains at Home 20

Glossary 22

Internet Sites 23

Index 24

The Berenstain Team

*S*tanley Berenstain and Janice Grant met on their first day of art school in 1941. They **admired** each other's artwork and soon became friends.

Stan and Jan discovered they both loved to draw comics. Each had their own painting style, but their cartoons were similar. After they married, Stan and Jan started working together.

Working as a team, they created cartoons for magazines. Then they began to write **humorous** books for adults. After awhile, they decided they wanted to write children's books.

Stan and Jan put a lot of thought into their first children's book. After much hard work, they created one of the most beloved families, the Berenstain Bears.

The Berenstains **published** their first bear book in 1962. Today, children still enjoy reading about the adventures of Mama, Papa, Sister, and Brother. The funny, easy-to-read stories have become favorites of many young readers.

Stan and Jan Berenstain have worked as a team for more than 50 years.

Stan Berenstain

Stanley Berenstain was born on September 29, 1923, in Philadelphia, Pennsylvania. As a child, he liked to draw pictures and read.

Stan's mother often gave him money to buy books at a used bookstore. He chose art **instruction** books and soon learned to draw his favorite comic strip character, Popeye. After high school, he went to the Philadelphia College of Art.

During **World War II**, Stan was **drafted** into the U.S. Army. For three years, he worked for a doctor. Stan made detailed drawings of **plastic surgeries**. He watched more than 3,000 operations.

When the war was over, Corporal Berenstain was offered another medical job. But he did not take it. He wanted to return home, marry Jan, and become a cartoonist.

Stan **submitted** four cartoons to a magazine called the *Saturday Review of Literature*. They bought the cartoons for $35 each. "It doesn't sound like a lot of money," Stan said, "but back then it was a huge amount. The army paid me $40 a month." This was the start of the couple's **professional** career.

Stanley Berenstain, 1943

Jan Berenstain

*J*anice Grant Berenstain was born on July 26, 1923, in Philadelphia, Pennsylvania. She was the middle child between two brothers.

Jan always loved to draw. Her father had studied art. He had an **easel** and **drafting table** set up in the house. Jan liked to sit beside him and draw on his scrap paper. Once she traced a drawing on the tissue paper in his favorite book, *Alice in Wonderland*. But he didn't punish her.

Jan enjoyed the Sunday comics. In her early teens, she sent some of her own cartoons to *Collier's* magazine. They **rejected** the cartoons. But her family **encouraged** her to continue drawing.

Opposite Page: Janice Grant, 1943

Jan decided to go to the school her father had attended, the Philadelphia College of Art. During **World War II**, she left school to work as a **riveter** in an airplane factory. She and Stan wrote to each other often. After the war, Jan returned to art school and married Stan.

Early Work

*T*he Berenstains were **determined** to succeed as artists. They worked hard, using a team system. One would draw a picture and the other would write a funny **caption**. They created 20 cartoons a week. But no one would buy them.

Nearly a year passed before the Berenstains finally made a sale to *Collier's* magazine. After their cartoons appeared in *Collier's*, many other magazines accepted the Berenstains' work. Soon, they were making enough money to buy a new house in the **suburbs** of Philadelphia.

During this time, the Berenstains' family began to grow. Their son Leo was born in 1948. Three years later, their second son, Michael, was born.

In 1951, the Berenstains **published** their first book. It was called *The Berenstains' Baby Book*. It was a **humorous** book written for adults. The book was about a subject familiar to the Berenstains, taking care of babies.

This was a busy time for the Berenstains. They wrote several **humorous** books and taught a children's art class at the Philadelphia Settlement School of Music and Art.

Today, the Berenstains still use the team system that made them successful in the late 1940s.

It's All in the Family

*I*n 1956, the Berenstains began to write an illustrated **feature** for *McCall's* magazine called "It's All in the Family." It ran in the magazine for 14 years. Then, another magazine called *Good Housekeeping* **published** it until 1989.

The couple was rated among the top cartoonists in the country. They did artwork for magazine covers. They illustrated books and ads. They created calendars and greeting cards for Hallmark. A book of the "It's All in the Family" cartoons was published in 1958, followed by another one called *It's Still in the Family*.

Soon, the Berenstains became interested in writing children's books. With two young readers of their own, they were especially interested in books that would help children learn to read.

The Berenstains' kids loved stories about animals. So, they decided to write a storybook about a bear family from Bear

Country. It was called *Freddy Bear's Spanking*. They took it to Beginner Books. This company was run by Theodor Geisel, better-known as Dr. Seuss.

Sons Leo (above, left) and Michael (below, left) inspired the Berenstains to write fun, educational books for children.

The Birth of the Bears

*D*r. Seuss liked the Berenstains' bear story but suggested many changes. They rewrote it six times! When *The Big Honey Hunt* was **published** in 1962, the story had completely changed.

Next, Dr. Seuss suggested they try a book about a different animal. So the Berenstains wrote a story called *Nothing Ever Happens at the South Pole*. It was about a penguin.

In the meantime, the Berenstains' bear book had become a best-seller. So, Dr. Seuss changed his mind. He asked for more stories about the bear family. The penguin tale was never published.

In the Berenstains' second book, *The Bike Lesson*, Dr. Seuss named the furry family "The Berenstain Bears." He also shortened the authors' names from Stanley and Janice to Stan and Jan. This allowed their **byline** to fit on the book's cover.

The early books had only three characters. The Berenstains decided to add a baby sister to the family in 1974. By then, Stan and Jan were writing four or five books every year.

The Berenstain Bears use humor to teach kids about life's ups and downs.

About the Bears

*B*efore long, the Berenstain Bears had grown popular among young readers. Fans could find the Berenstain Bears in coloring books, on a TV cartoon series, and in holiday specials.

The books had become so popular that the Berenstains began to write even more stories. They created Berenstain Bear books for different reading levels. They wrote books for toddlers, and created their Big Chapter Books for older children.

Readers often ask the Berenstains why they only write about bears. "We chose bears because they can stand up and they look good in clothes and are fun to draw," they answer.

The Berenstains decided that bear family's ages would never change. Papa and Mama are in their thirties. Brother Bear is in fourth grade and Sister Bear is in second grade.

The authors get many ideas for the books from their own children and grandchildren. For example, *The Bike Lesson* was based on helping one of their sons learn to ride a two-wheeler.

Other titles deal with things that children often experience, such as having a bad dream, arguing with a family member, or going to the dentist. But not all of the books are lessons. Some are just meant to be fun and to help children learn to read.

The Berenstains draw their bears using waterproof ink and watercolors.

Working Together

*T*he Berenstains always share the work when they create the books. Both think up story ideas and write the words. Stan's favorite place to write is at the dining room table. Jan's favorite place is in an easy chair in the breakfast **nook**.

After the writing is complete, the artwork begins. "Stan is very good at laying out the whole book," Jan says, "and I'm very good at drawing the characters. Usually, he draws the background and places the characters, and then I develop them. Finally, the coloring of the book is shared."

It takes about three months of working every day to finish a book. Drawing takes more time than writing. Stan likes to draw **humorous** subjects. Jan is more serious. Both agree that all the books must be funny.

Today, the Berenstains' sons work on the Big Chapter Books with them. Leo does the writing with help from Stan. Michael does the cover and illustrations with Jan's help.

Stan, Jan, Leo, and Michael pose with their first Big Chapter Book, **The Berenstain Bears and the Drug Free Zone.**

The Berenstains at Home

*J*an and Stan live in a large house on a hill in the Pennsylvania woods. When they look out the window, what they see looks very much like Bear Country. There are lots of trees and big red barns.

When they're not working, the Berenstains like to spend time with their four grandchildren. They also like to read. Stan usually chooses biographies and history books. Jan prefers mysteries and detective stories. Stan is also a sports fan. He likes watching the Philadelphia Eagles football team.

The Berenstains are able to slow their work pace now that their sons help them with the books. But Jan and Stan still enjoy creating the books and say, "We're going to keep on doing it until we get it wrong."

The Berenstains hard at work in their Pennsylvania studio

Glossary

admire - to have respect for something.

byline - an author's name on a book or article.

caption - a written description of a cartoon or photograph.

determined - to make up one's mind very firmly.

draft - to be selected for military service. People who are drafted must serve in the armed forces.

drafting table - a large, upright table used for drawing and sketching.

easel - a standing framework which holds a painter's canvas.

encourage - to give hope to someone.

feature - a story, article, or cartoon that gets special attention.

humorous - something that is funny or amusing.

instruction - the act of teaching someone something.

nook - a small corner.

plastic surgery - an operation to rebuild parts of the face or body that are damaged.

professional - working for money rather than for pleasure.

publish - to produce and offer printed materials for sale to the public.

reject - to refuse to take something.

riveter - person who fastens metal bolts into a piece of equipment.

submit - to send work to a publisher in hopes that he or she will buy it.

suburbs - a housing area near the outskirts of a city.

World War II - 1939 to 1945, fought in Europe, Asia, and Africa. The United States, France, Great Britain, the Soviet Union, and their allies were on one side. Germany, Italy, Japan, and their allies were on the other side. The war began when Germany invaded Poland. America entered the war in 1941 after Japan bombed Pearl Harbor, Hawaii.

Internet Sites

The Official Berenstain Bears Web site
http://www.berenstainbears.com

Spend time learning about the Berenstain Bears on their official Web site. While there, you can read an interactive storybook, create your own Berenstain Bears coloring book, take a tour of the Berenstain Bears' tree house, and much more. This site also has a place where Jan and Stan Berenstain answer young readers' questions.

Special thanks to Stan and Jan Berenstain for their invaluable assistance with this project.

Index

B

Berenstain, Leo (son) 10, 18

Berenstain, Michael (son) 10, 18

Berenstains' Baby Book, The 10

Big Chapter Books 16, 18

Big Honey Hunt, The 14

Bike Lesson, The 14, 16

books 4, 10, 11, 12, 15, 16, 17, 18

Brother Bear 4, 16

C

cartoons 4, 7, 8, 10, 12

Collier's magazine 8, 10

D

Dr. Seuss 13, 14

F

Freddy Bear's Spanking 13

G

Good Housekeeping magazine 12

I

"It's All in the Family" 12

It's Still in the Family 12

M

Mama Bear 4, 16

McCall's magazine 12

N

Nothing Ever Happens at the South Pole 14

P

Papa Bear 4, 16

Philadelphia College of Art 6, 9

Philadelphia Settlement School of Music and Art 11

S

Saturday Review of Literature 7

Sister Bear 4, 15, 16

W

World War II 6, 9